Maritime 123

a counting book from Canada

written and illustrated by
J.R.Mason-Browne

FOUR
EAST
PUBLICATIONS

When you are in the Maritimes

you can see...

1 Wet whale

near Grand Manan Island, NB.

2 Turtles turn in

Kejimkujik Park, NS.

3 Moose meet

near Moncton, NB.

4

Furry foxes from

Lennox Island, PEI.

5 Funny frogs

 in Pugwash, NS.

6 Silly seals swim

under Confederation Bridge.

7 Lobsters let loose

in Lunenburg, NS.

8 Crows come calling

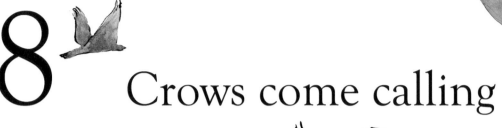

over Summerside, PEI.

9

Flying fish frolic

in Chéticamp, NS.

10 Ducks drift down

the Saint John River.

11 Gulls gather

over Borden, PEI.

12 Jellyfish jiggle

in Baie Verte.

13 Green grasshoppers gather

around Ross Farm, NS.

14 Plovers play

in Cavendish, PEI.

15 Deer drink

near Alma, NB.

16 Cows chew

in Sussex, NB.

17 Sheep stand still

in Baddeck, NS.

18 Seashells scattered

along the Fundy Shore.

19 Beautiful bugs

in Montague, PEI.

20 Horses hurry home

on Sable Island.

Wow!

That's a lot of animals!

1 one

2 two

3 three

4 four

5 five

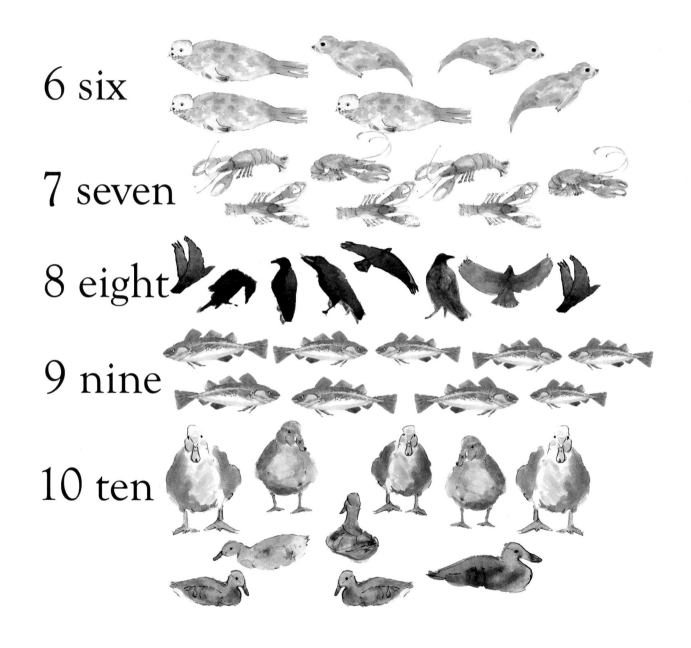

6 six

7 seven

8 eight

9 nine

10 ten

11 eleven

12 twelve

13 thirteen

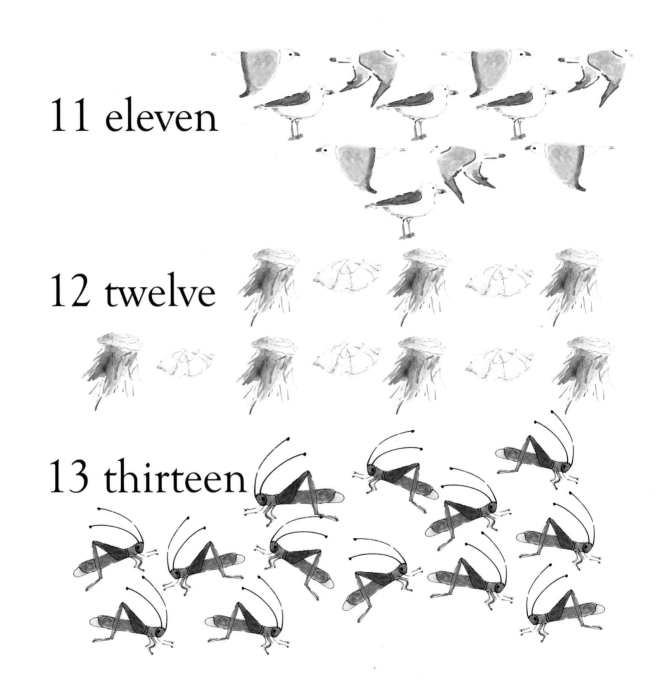

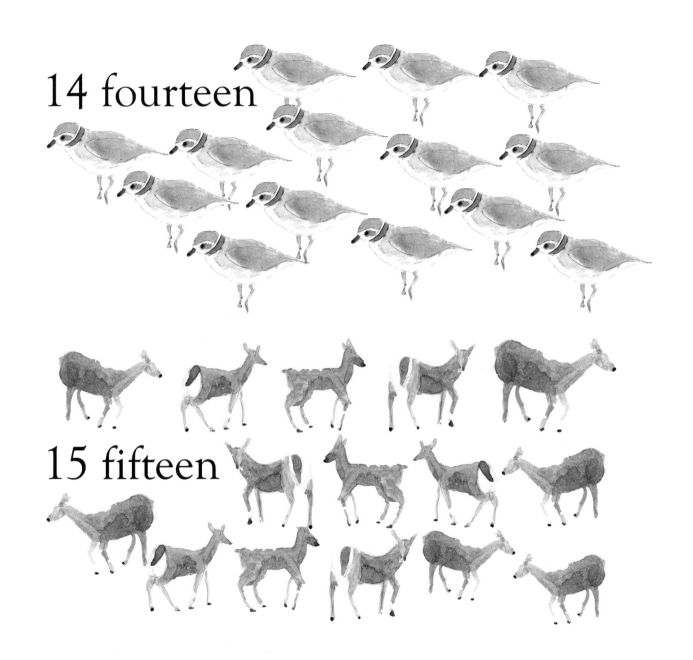

14 fourteen

15 fifteen

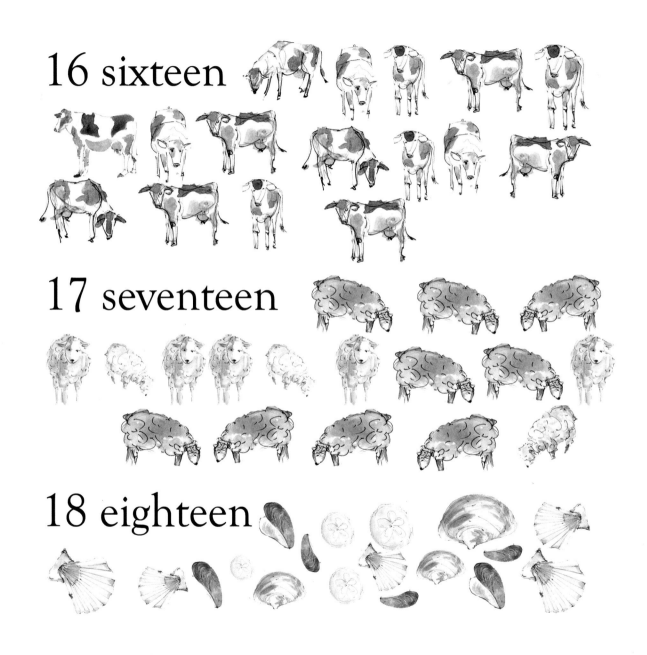

16 sixteen

17 seventeen

18 eighteen

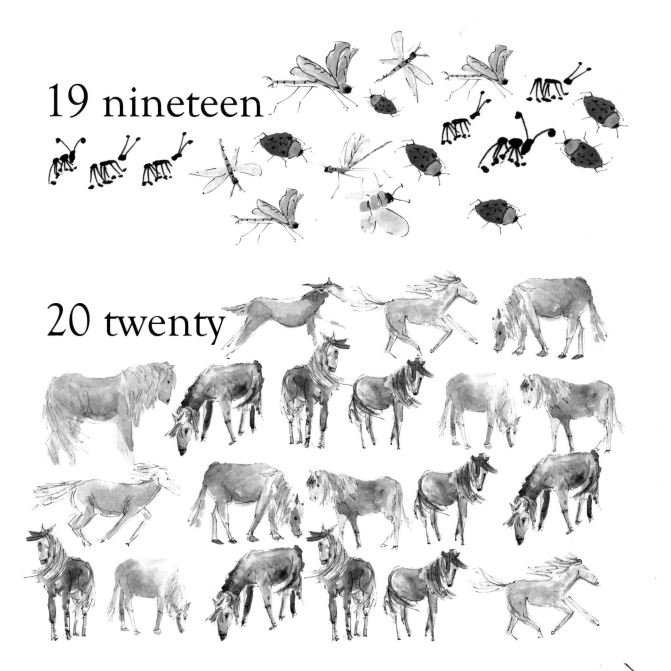

19 nineteen

20 twenty

For the boys;
Rhys, Elliot, Byron, and Owen

editing by Grayce Rogers
text and cover layout and design by J.R. Mason-Browne
Printed and bound in Canada
This is a work of fiction.
Any resemblance to actual events or persons, living or dead, is purely coincidental.

Published in Canada by Four East Publications
P.O. Box 3087 Tantallon, Nova Scotia B3Z 4G9
www.glenmargaret.com
Library and Archives of Canada Cataloguing in Publication
Mason-Browne, Jane, 1958-
Maritime 123 / J.R. Mason-Browne.
ISBN 978-1-897462-13-3
1. Counting-Juvenile literature. 2. Maritime
Provinces - Pictorial works- Juvenile literature.
I. title. II. Title: Maritime one, two, three
QA113.M376 2010   j513.2'11   C2010-904208-5